Fashion BLOG Planner journal

Kaylee Berry

Weston Tree Publishing

First printing: November 2017

Cover photo from Freepik.com

All quotes, except for the authors personal ones, were taken from BrainyQuote.com

ISBN: 978-1-948335-01-0

Dedication

To all my fellow bloggers.
May we have success in all we write, create,
plan and propose.
I look forward to reading all that comes out of your journal.

Table of Contents

HOW TO USE THIS BOOK

Reader Profile

Use the reader profile to get to know your ideal audience. Fill in every blank to create a complete guide of who your readers are, what they like, and what they want from you.

Writing Tips

Read over the tips in this section often to keep your writing interesting and engaging. It will help you to focus on your readers as you write and therefore create better content.

One Year - One Post a Week Schedule

For most blogs one post a week is enough. Use this one-year planner to come up with a theme for each month. Then plan your posts out for each week. For your convenience 5 weeks are included in case you post on a certain day of the week and there happen to be 5 in a month. You will be able to see a whole years worth of content at a glance.

Post Publishing Checklist

Use this helpful checklist every time you get ready to publish a new post. It has all the steps you need to successfully launch a new post. As a bonus there is an additional checklist of extra ways to create more content using your post.

Journal Pages

Use this journal to collect all your *never-ending* ideas. There is room to write about ways to grow your blog, products to launch, and ideas for posts. If you're ever stuck use the prompts to inspire you. In this section of the book you'll also find a page to record "What I Wore Today" with a sketch box for drawing outfits or adding a photo. You'll also find inspirational quotes to keep you motivated to write, grow your blog, and find success.

Index

Every journal entry has a place to fill in a category. This will allow you to easily categorize your ideas for quick reference later. The index has room for thirteen categories and room enough to write every page number that corresponds with that idea.

IN ORDER TO
HAVE AN AUDIENCE,
YOU MUST WRITE FOR ONE.

-Kaylee Berry

IDEAL READER PROFILE

Name: ____

Age: ____

Location: ____

Occupation: ____

Relationship Status: ___________________________________

Religious Preferences: _________________________________

Hobbies: ____

____

Interests: ____

____

What are they looking to gain from your blog? _______________

____

____

What do they spend time online doing? ______________________

____

____

Where do they shop? ___________________________________

____

____

IDEAL READER PROFILE CONT.

Describe their general disposition and personality: ______________________

____

____

____

What activities would fill their calendar for the next year? ______________

____

____

____

What influences their buying decisions? ____________________________

____

What would make them trust and respect you? ______________________

____

____

Would they ever spend money on services/products you offer? __________

____

____

What would it take for them to purchase them from you? ______________

____

____

What questions would they ask you if they sat across from you drinking coffee? ____

____

____

____

____

____

THREE QUESTIONS

Ask yourself these questions before you start writing....

Question 1: What am I writing about?

Choose a theme and main topic. Don't try to cram too many things in a single post. Have no more than two sub-points. Otherwise, it will be hard for your readers to follow along.

Question 2: What am I trying to say?

Know which side of the argument you are on. Choose a simple statement that you can easily remember. Write it down next to your workspace and refer to it often. It will be what you base every writing decision on. Think of it as your worldview.

Ex. I believe all people have the right to work at a job that they love.

Ex. All women deserve to feel beautifulin their own skin.

Use your "writers statement" to build all of your content. It will be what you are known for.

Question 3: Who am I writing for?

Imagine your ideal reader every time you form a sentence. Think about how they will receive your words. Try to give them what they want. Entertain them, inspire them, move them to have strong emotions, or whatever your goal is in your writing.

Writing Tips

Put Your Readers First

In order to have an audience, you must write for one. You must think about your reader with every word you write. Picture them receiving your ideas, being entertained by your words, finding inspiration in your stories.

Your audience is your number one priority when you write. Whether you're trying to get your reader to spend some of their hard earned money on your book, trying to teach them something, or sharing your experiences to help others going through a similar situation, you must build trust.

They need to know that you have their best interests at heart. They are looking for someone who is genuine and sharing something that interests them. Your audience wants to be entertained, taught, and inspired. Be the kind of writer that delivers what they want.

Be a Thought Leader

The key to having raving fans is to have killer content. Every word out of your mouth should be prophetic.

Your focus should be on producing something that is life changing to anyone who reads it. Filler and fluff just won't cut it. Use your words to inspire others, and they will inspire others with your words.

When you hear or see something amazing, you want to share it with everyone you know. Your following may start out small, but it will grow over time by people sharing what you say.

It takes more than just experience to be a thought leader. It takes stepping out of the norm and thinking outside of the box. It's a combination of mastery and continual searching. There is still much to be discovered. Be a pioneer. Then report back to everyone the wonderful things you've found.

Show Your Audience You're a Real Person

Let your readers get to know the real you. Tell them stories from your life to help them connect with you. Share your struggles and joys.

Bring your personality to whatever you're writing. Don't hide behind your keyboard and create a persona that doesn't represent you. Use words that you would use in everyday conversation. Slip in a bit of your sense of humor.

Give your readers permission to talk to you directly. In fact, ask them to. At the end of posts or emails, encourage them to respond directly to you. If people like you and get to know you, they will trust you.

Write Like You're Talking to a Friend

Picture yourself dialoguing with your best friend or your ideal reader. Use words and phrases you would use in real conversations. Let the conversation flow from one topic to the next.

When you are with a friend, you're not nervous or self-conscious. You are at ease and feel safe. Your writing should convey those things. Show your readers you are comfortable with them.

Open up to them and let them know your secrets. Create inside jokes that only your readers will understand. You want to build community among the people you write for. They will sense your authenticity and be drawn to you and your work.

Share Your Unique Perspective

You may be thinking to yourself, "There are already a ton of blogs out there. Why would anyone want to read mine?" I personally think there could never be enough blogs. Every writer has their own voice and style that is different from any other. What speaks to one person won't have the same effect on the next. That is why the world needs your voice, to reach others like you.

Whatever interests you, most likely interests other people too. So share your unique perspective, and you will find *your* people. Your distinct approach and knowledge on a specific subject will be unique and put you above the rest.

Make It Interesting

Facts and figures are necessary for some audiences. I understand that, but if you don't make your content interesting and lively readers will pass over your work.

Use things we've talked about like personal stories, your unique take on things, writing like you're talking with a friend, using plain language, adding a bit of your humor.

You can break up text with quote or pictures to make your posts more reader-friendly and break up the large sections of text. Doing this will help to keep your readers attention.

Find Your Voice

Decide how you want to present your information. Are you going to be funny and humorous, sarcastic and snarky, gentle and kind, motherly, edgy? You decide what writing style best fits your personality and include it in every piece you write.

This will be your voice.

Final Thoughts

Writing to influence people can be a big responsibility so always aim to encourage and uplift and don't use your words to tear down.

When you think you've run out of ideas and inspiration for writing, commit to journaling every day. You'll be amazed at the thoughts you have when you give yourself some room to breathe and be creative.

ONE YEAR

ONE POST A WEEK PLANNER

One Year
One Post a Week Schedule

Month:________________ Theme:______________________

Post 1 ____
Post 2 ____
Post 3 ____
Post 4 ____
Post 5 ____

Month:________________ Theme:______________________

Post 1 ____
Post 2 ____
Post 3 ____
Post 4 ____
Post 5 ____

Month:________________ Theme:______________________

Post 1 ____
Post 2 ____
Post 3 ____
Post 4 ____
Post 5 ____

Month:________________ Theme:______________________

Post 1 ____
Post 2 ____
Post 3 ____
Post 4 ____
Post 5 ____

Month November Theme: Family/Gratitude
Post 1 What I'm most thankful for
Post 2 10 Ways to Cultivate Gratitude

Month:________________ Theme:________________

Post 1 ________________
Post 2 ________________
Post 3 ________________
Post 4 ________________
Post 5 ________________

Month:________________ Theme:________________

Post 1 ________________
Post 2 ________________
Post 3 ________________
Post 4 ________________
Post 5 ________________

Month:________________ Theme:________________

Post 1 ________________
Post 2 ________________
Post 3 ________________
Post 4 ________________
Post 5 ________________

Month:________________ Theme:________________

Post 1 ________________
Post 2 ________________
Post 3 ________________
Post 4 ________________
Post 5 ________________

Month:__________________ Theme:________________________

Post 1 ____
Post 2 ____
Post 3 ____
Post 4 ____
Post 5 ____

Month:__________________ Theme:________________________

Post 1 ____
Post 2 ____
Post 3 ____
Post 4 ____
Post 5 ____

Month:__________________ Theme:________________________

Post 1 ____
Post 2 ____
Post 3 ____
Post 4 ____
Post 5 ____

Month:__________________ Theme:________________________

Post 1 ____
Post 2 ____
Post 3 ____
Post 4 ____
Post 5 ____

Publishing Checklist & Headline Templates

Post Publishing Checklist

- ☐ Good Title that builds interest
- ☐ Researched
- ☐ Proofread
- ☐ Grammar Checked
- ☐ Tags added
- ☐ Link to Old Posts
- ☐ Add Feature Image
- ☐ Use Short Paragraphs
- ☐ Break up the text with Images
- ☐ Built in SEO (Search Engine Optimization)
- ☐ Call to Action
- ☐ Pull out quotes
- ☐ Highlight or Bold Important Sections for easy Skimming
- ☐ Share on Social Media Outlets

Create More Content by Re-purposing your Post

- ☐ Create a video
- ☐ Use it for a Podcast
- ☐ Turn it into a series
- ☐ Use it in a book
- ☐ Create a workbook/checklist/template
- ☐ Use the idea to create an E-Course

Blog Post Title/Headline Templates

(#) Easy Fixes to __________(fashion disaster)

Look and Feel Confident in _______________ (fashion trend)

My favorite trends of ____(season)

(#) ____ guaranteed to make your _____ easier

(#) Tips to Make Your Wardrobe Look Effortless

(#) Clever Tools to Simplify your _______

Think you know how to _______

How to _________ (beauty treatment) the right way

Are you making these _________ Mistakes?

Confessions of a ________

When you feel ________

Like _______? Then you'll Love This

(#)-Point Checklist

(#) Key Benefits of __________

Quick Guide to _________ (your best tip)

How to Get Your ___(part of your body) to __________

What to Wear to ________(special occasion)

(#) Rules for __________

The Do's and Don'ts of _________________

How to Feel _________ Wearing ____________

____

____

____

Share

your experiences with this blog planner
on social media.

#TheBlogThatNeverEnds

Title: ______________________________

Date / /

Category: ______________________________

What happened to me today that would be interesting/entertaining for my readers?

Notes:

☐Drafted ☐Proofread ☐Published

Title: ______________________________

Category: ______________________________

Date / /

What I Wore Today

Outfit: ______________________________

____

Accessories: ______________________________

Hair: ______________________________

Shoes: ______________________________

Makeup: ______________________________

How did it make me feel? ______________________________

____

____

☐Drafted ☐Proofread ☐Published

Title: ______________________________

Date / /

Category: ______________________________

What is my best fashion advice?

Notes: ______________________________

☐Drafted ☐Proofread ☐Published

Title: ____________________

Date / /

Category: ____________________

WORDS ARE THE MEDIUM BY WHICH WRITERS CREATE.

-Kaylee Berry

☐Drafted ☐Proofread ☐Published

Title: ______________________________

Date / /

Category: ______________________________

What is something about myself that I've never shared with my readers before?

Notes: ______________________________

☐Drafted ☐Proofread ☐Published

Title: ______________________________

Category: ______________________________

Date / /

What I Wore Today

Outfit: ____

____

Accessories: ____

Hair: ____

Shoes: ____

Makeup: ____

How did it make me feel? ______________________________

____

____

☐Drafted ☐Proofread ☐Published

Title: ______________________________

Date / /

Category: ______________________________

What is on my mind today that I can't stop thinking about?

Notes: ______________________________

☐Drafted ☐Proofread ☐Published

Title: ______________________________

Date / /

Category: ______________________________

FASHION IS NOT SOMETHING THAT EXISTS IN DRESSES ONLY. FASHION IS IN THE SKY, IN THE STREET, FASHION HAS TO DO WITH IDEAS, THE WAY WE LIVE, WHAT IS HAPPENING.

-Coco Chanel

☐Drafted ☐Proofread ☐Published

Title: ______________________________

Date / /

Category: ______________________________

Why did I start writing my blog in the first place?

Notes: ______________________________

☐Drafted ☐Proofread ☐Published

Title: ______________________________

Category: ______________________________

Date / /

What I Wore Today

Outfit: ____

____

Accessories: ____

Hair: ____

Shoes: ____

Makeup: ____

How did it make me feel? ______________________________

____

____

☐Drafted ☐Proofread ☐Published

Title: ______________________________

Category: ______________________________

Date / /

What pieces could I not live without in my wardrobe?

Notes: ______________________________

☐Drafted ☐Proofread ☐Published

Title: ______________________________

Category: ___________________________

Date / /

SUCCESS IS NO ACCIDENT. IT IS HARD WORK, PERSEVERANCE, LEARNING, STUDYING, SACRIFICE AND MOST OF ALL, LOVE OF WHAT YOU ARE DOING OR LEARNING TO DO.

-Pele

☐Drafted ☐Proofread ☐Published

Title: ______________________________

Date / /

Category: ______________________________

Why do I love blogging?

Notes: ______________________________

☐Drafted ☐Proofread ☐Published

Title: ______________________________

Category: ______________________________

Date / /

What I Wore Today

Outfit: ______________________________

____

Accessories: ______________________________

Hair: ______________________________

Shoes: ______________________________

Makeup: ______________________________

How did it make me feel? ______________________________

____

____

☐Drafted ☐Proofread ☐Published

Title: ______________________________

Date / /

Category: ______________________________

What is something new I'd like to try?

Notes: ______________________________

☐Drafted ☐Proofread ☐Published

Title: ______________________________

Date / /

Category: ______________________________

EITHER WRITE SOMETHING WORTH READING OR DO SOMETHING WORTH WRITING.

-*Benjamin Franklin*

☐Drafted ☐Proofread ☐Published

Title: ______________________________

Date / /

Category: ______________________________

What does my audience want from me?

Notes: ______________________________

☐Drafted ☐Proofread ☐Published

Title: ______________________________

Category: ______________________________

Date / /

What I Wore Today

Outfit: ______________________________

____

Accessories: ______________________________

Hair: ______________________________

Shoes: ______________________________

Makeup: ______________________________

How did it make me feel? ______________________________

____

____

☐Drafted ☐Proofread ☐Published

Title: ______________________________

Category: ______________________________

Date / /

What does my look say about me?

Notes: ______________________________

☐Drafted ☐Proofread ☐Published

Title: ______________________________

Category: ______________________________

Date / /

I DO NOT SEE THE PROCESS OF BLOGGING AS A SEPARATE THING FROM CREATING ART. THIS IS IN PART WHY I DO NOT LIKE TO BE KNOWN FOR BEING A 'BLOGGER,' AS THIS IS JUST ONE FORM OF OUTPUT FOR CREATIVE IDEAS.

-Keri Smith

☐Drafted ☐Proofread ☐Published

Title: ______________________________

Date / /

Category: ______________________________

How can I be a more effective communicator?

Notes: ______________________________

☐Drafted ☐Proofread ☐Published

Title: ______________________________

Category: ______________________________

Date / /

What I Wore Today

Outfit: ____

____

Accessories: ____

Hair: ____

Shoes: ____

Makeup: ____

How did it make me feel? ______________________________

____

____

❒Drafted ❒Proofread ❒Published

Title: ______________________________

Date / /

Category:______________________________

Who is my favorite blogger and why?

Notes:______________________________

☐Drafted ☐Proofread ☐Published

Title: ______________________________

Category: ___________________________

Date / /

FASHION IS ABOUT DRESSING ACCORDING TO WHAT'S FASHIONABLE. STYLE IS MORE ABOUT BEING YOURSELF.

-Oscar de la Renta

☐Drafted ☐Proofread ☐Published

Title: ______________________________

Category: ______________________________

Date / /

What is my go-to outfit?

Notes: ______________________________

☐Drafted ☐Proofread ☐Published

Title: ______________________________

Date / /

Category: ______________________________

What I Wore Today

Outfit: ______________________________

____

Accessories: ______________________________

Hair: ______________________________

Shoes: ______________________________

Makeup: ______________________________

How did it make me feel? ______________________________

____

____

☐Drafted ☐Proofread ☐Published

Title: ______________________________

Date / /

Category: ______________________________

What would be my advice to someone just starting out in the fashion world?

Notes: ______________________________

☐Drafted ☐Proofread ☐Published

Title: ______________________________

Category: ___________________________

Date / /

YOUR POSITIVE ACTION COMBINED WITH POSITIVE THINKING RESULTS IN SUCCESS.

-Shiv Khera

☐Drafted ☐Proofread ☐Published

Title: ____________________

Date / /

Category: ____________________

What is my favorite part of being a blogger?

Notes: ____________________

☐Drafted ☐Proofread ☐Published

Title: ______________________________

Category: ______________________________

Date / /

What I Wore Today

Outfit: ______________________________

____

Accessories: ______________________________

Hair: ______________________________

Shoes: ______________________________

Makeup: ______________________________

How did it make me feel? ______________________________

____

____

☐Drafted ☐Proofread ☐Published

Title: ______________________________

Date / /

Category: ______________________________

What area of blogging do I struggle with most?

Notes: ______________________________

☐Drafted ☐Proofread ☐Published

Title: ______________________

Category: ______________________

Date / /

BE SURE WHAT YOU WANT AND BE SURE ABOUT YOURSELF. FASHION IS NOT JUST BEAUTY, IT'S ABOUT GOOD ATTITUDE. YOU HAVE TO BELIEVE IN YOURSELF AND BE STRONG.

-Adriana Lima

☐Drafted ☐Proofread ☐Published

Title: ______________________

Category: ______________________

Date / /

What advice would I give to my younger self?

Notes: ______________________

☐Drafted ☐Proofread ☐Published

Title: ______________________________

Category: ______________________________

Date / /

What I Wore Today

Outfit: ______________________________

____

Accessories: ______________________________

Hair: ______________________________

Shoes: ______________________________

Makeup: ______________________________

How did it make me feel? ______________________________

____

____

☐Drafted ☐Proofread ☐Published

Title: ______________________________

Date / /

Category: ______________________________

What have I read recently that inspired me?

Notes: ______________________________

☐Drafted ☐Proofread ☐Published

Title: ______________________________

Category: ______________________________

Date / /

FASHION
IS ABOUT
DREAMING AND
MAKING OTHER
PEOPLE DREAM.

-Donatella Versace

☐Drafted ☐Proofread ☐Published

Title: ______________________________

Date / /

Category: ______________________________

How can I help my readers in the areas that they are interested in?

Notes: ______________________________

☐Drafted ☐Proofread ☐Published

Title: ______________________________

Category: ______________________________

Date / /

What I Wore Today

Outfit: ______________________________

____

Accessories: ______________________________

Hair: ______________________________

Shoes: ______________________________

Makeup: ______________________________

How did it make me feel? ______________________________

____

____

☐Drafted ☐Proofread ☐Published

Title: ____________________

Date / /

Category: ____________________

What could I teach my audience?

Notes: ____________________

☐Drafted ☐Proofread ☐Published

Title: ______________________________

Date / /

Category: ______________________________

SOME PEOPLE DREAM OF SUCCESS, WHILE OTHER PEOPLE GET UP EVERY MORNING AND MAKE IT HAPPEN.

-Wayne Huizenga

☐Drafted ☐Proofread ☐Published

Title: ______________________

Category: ______________________

Date / /

What is my biggest struggle in life?

Notes: ______________________

☐Drafted ☐Proofread ☐Published

Title: ______________________________

Date / /

Category: ______________________________

What I Wore Today

Outfit: ______________________________

____

Accessories: ______________________________

Hair: ______________________________

Shoes: ______________________________

Makeup: ______________________________

How did it make me feel? ______________________________

____

____

☐Drafted ☐Proofread ☐Published

Title: ______________________

Date / /

Category: ______________________

What do my readers struggle with?

Notes: ______________________

☐Drafted ☐Proofread ☐Published

Title: ______________________________

Date / /

Category: ______________________________

HABITS LIKE BLOGGING OFTEN AND REGULARLY, WRITING DOWN THE WAY YOU THINK, BEING CLEAR ABOUT WHAT YOU THINK ARE EFFECTIVE TACTICS, IGNORING THE BURBLING CROWD ...ALL OF THESE ARE USEFUL HABITS.

-Seth Godin

☐Drafted ☐Proofread ☐Published

Title: ______________________________

Date / /

Category: ______________________________

What marketing ideas do I have for my blog?

Notes: ______________________________

☐Drafted ☐Proofread ☐Published

Title: ______________________________

Category: ______________________________

Date / /

What I Wore Today

Outfit: ______________________________

____

Accessories: ______________________________

Hair: ______________________________

Shoes: ______________________________

Makeup: ______________________________

How did it make me feel? ______________________________

____

____

☐Drafted ☐Proofread ☐Published

Title: ______________________________

Date / /

Category: ______________________________

What do I want my brand to stand for?

Notes: ______________________________

☐Drafted ☐Proofread ☐Published

Title: ______________________________

Category: ____________________________

Date / /

WRITING, TO ME, IS SIMPLY THINKING THROUGH MY FINGERS.

-Isaac Asimov

☐Drafted ☐Proofread ☐Published

Title: ______________________________

Date / /

Category: ____________________________

If I were to start another blog what would it be about?

Notes: ______________________________

☐Drafted ☐Proofread ☐Published

Title: ______________________________

Date / /

Category: ____________________________

What I Wore Today

Outfit: ____

____

Accessories: ____

Hair: ____

Shoes: ____

Makeup: ____

How did it make me feel? ___________________________

____

____

☐Drafted ☐Proofread ☐Published

Title: ______________________

Date / /

Category: ______________________

What trend have I put off accepting and why?

Notes: ______________________

☐Drafted ☐Proofread ☐Published

Title: ______________________________

Category: ______________________________

Date / /

YOUR WRITING VOICE IS THE DEEPEST POSSIBLE REFLECTION OF WHO YOU ARE.... IN YOUR VOICE, YOUR READERS SHOULD BE ABLE TO HEAR THE CONTENTS OF YOUR MIND, YOUR HEART, YOUR SOUL.

-Meg Rosoff

☐Drafted ☐Proofread ☐Published

Title: ______________________

Date / /

Category: ______________________

How can I insert my unique voice and perspective into the article I'm currently working on?

Notes: ______________________

☐Drafted ☐Proofread ☐Published

Title: ______________________________

Category: ______________________________

Date / /

What I Wore Today

Outfit: ______________________________

____

Accessories: ______________________________

Hair: ______________________________

Shoes: ______________________________

Makeup: ______________________________

How did it make me feel? ______________________________

____

____

☐Drafted ☐Proofread ☐Published

Title: ______________________________

Date / /

Category: ____________________________

Write up a proposal to publish a guest post on your favorite blog?

Notes: ________________________________

☐Drafted ☐Proofread ☐Published

Title: ______________________________

Date / /

Category: ______________________________

THESE DAYS, YOU HAVE THE OPTION OF STAYING HOME, BLOGGING IN YOUR UNDERWEAR, AND NOT HAVING YOUR WORDS MANGLED. I THINK I LIKE THE DIRECTION THINGS ARE HEADED.

-Marc Andreessen

☐Drafted ☐Proofread ☐Published

Title: ______________________________ Date / /

Category: ______________________________

Where do I draw my inspiration from for my wardrobe?

Notes: ______________________________

☐Drafted ☐Proofread ☐Published

Title: ______________________________

Category: ______________________________

Date / /

What I Wore Today

Outfit: ______________________________

____

Accessories: ______________________________

Hair: ______________________________

Shoes: ______________________________

Makeup: ______________________________

How did it make me feel? ______________________________

____

____

☐Drafted ☐Proofread ☐Published

Title: ______________________________

Date / /

Category: ______________________________

What is my best fashion hack?

Notes: ______________________________

☐Drafted ☐Proofread ☐Published

Title: ______________________________

Date / /

Category: ______________________________

HAPPINESS LIES IN THE JOY OF ACHIEVEMENT AND THE THRILL OF CREATIVE EFFORT.

-Franklin D. Roosevelt

☐Drafted ☐Proofread ☐Published

Title: ______________________________

Date / /

Category: ____________________________

Go learn something about blogging today. Then write down what your biggest takeaways were.

Notes: ______________________________

☐Drafted ☐Proofread ☐Published

Title: ______________________________

Category: ____________________________

Date / /

What I Wore Today

Outfit: ______________________________

____

Accessories: ______________________________

Hair: ______________________________

Shoes: ______________________________

Makeup: ______________________________

How did it make me feel? ______________________________

____

____

☐Drafted ☐Proofread ☐Published

Title: ______________________________ Date / /

Category: ______________________________

Does my branding need updating? Brainstorm ideas below.

Notes: ______________________________

☐Drafted ☐Proofread ☐Published

Title: ______________________________

Category: ______________________________

Date / /

SUCCESS ISN'T ALWAYS ABOUT GREATNESS. IT'S ABOUT CONSISTENCY. CONSISTENT HARD WORK LEADS TO SUCCESS. GREATNESS WILL COME.

-Dwayne Johnson

☐Drafted ☐Proofread ☐Published

Title: ______________________________

Date / /

Category: ____________________________

Tell your readers about your day? Do you have a routine you follow?

Notes: ______________________________

☐Drafted ☐Proofread ☐Published

Title: ______________________________

Category: ______________________________

Date   /   /

What I Wore Today

Outfit: ______________________________

____

Accessories: ______________________________

Hair: ______________________________

Shoes: ______________________________

Makeup: ______________________________

How did it make me feel? ______________________________

____

____

☐Drafted ☐Proofread ☐Published

Title: ________________________________

Date / /

Category: ________________________________

Visualize your blog being a success. What does that look like to you?

Notes: ________________________________

☐Drafted ☐Proofread ☐Published

Title: ______________________________

Date / /

Category: ______________________________

A MILLION AND ONE THOUGHTS FLY THROUGH MY BRAIN EVERY DAY. IF I DON'T WRITE SOME OF THEM DOWN BRILLIANT IDEAS COULD BE LOST.

-Kaylee Berry

☐Drafted ☐Proofread ☐Published

Title: ______________________

Date / /

Category: ______________________

Who has been a mentor to me and what have they taught me?

Notes: ______________________

☐Drafted ☐Proofread ☐Published

Title: ______________________

Category: ______________________

Date / /

What I Wore Today

Outfit: ______________________

____

Accessories: ______________________

Hair: ______________________

Shoes: ______________________

Makeup: ______________________

How did it make me feel? ______________________

____

____

☐Drafted ☐Proofread ☐Published

Title: ______________________

Date / /

Category: ______________________

What is consuming my thoughts today?

Notes: ______________________

☐Drafted ☐Proofread ☐Published

Title: ______________________________

Date / /

Category: ______________________________

CLOTHES IS JUST SOMETHING YOU PUT ON TO COVER YOURSELF... FASHION IS A WAY TO COMMUNICATE.

-Dries van Noten

☐Drafted ☐Proofread ☐Published

Title: ______________________________

Date / /

Category: ______________________________

What would I like to do a series of blog posts on?

Notes: ______________________________

☐Drafted ☐Proofread ☐Published

Title: ______________________________

Category: ______________________________

Date / /

What I Wore Today

Outfit: ______________________________

____

Accessories: ______________________________

Hair: ______________________________

Shoes: ______________________________

Makeup: ______________________________

How did it make me feel? ______________________________

____

____

☐Drafted ☐Proofread ☐Published

Title: ________________________

Date / /

Category: ________________________

What is something I would like to do, but feel like it's out of my comfort zone?

Notes: ________________________

☐Drafted ☐Proofread ☐Published

Title: ______________________________

Category: ___________________________

Date / /

THE BEST
FASHION SHOW
IS DEFINITELY
ON THE STREET.
ALWAYS HAS BEEN,
AND ALWAYS
WILL BE.

-Bill Cunningham

☐Drafted ☐Proofread ☐Published

Title: ______________________________

Date / /

Category: ____________________________

Who would I like to collaborate with on a product or giveaway?

Notes: ______________________________

☐Drafted ☐Proofread ☐Published

Title: ______________________________

Category: ______________________________

Date / /

What I Wore Today

Outfit: ______________________________

____

Accessories: ______________________________

Hair: ______________________________

Shoes: ______________________________

Makeup: ______________________________

How did it make me feel? ______________________________

____

____

☐Drafted ☐Proofread ☐Published

Title: ______________________________

Date / /

Category: ____________________________

How can I grow my email list this month?

Notes:

☐Drafted ☐Proofread ☐Published

Title: ______________________________

Date / /

Category: ______________________________

SUCCESS IS NOT THE KEY TO HAPPINESS. HAPPINESS IS THE KEY TO SUCCESS. IF YOU LOVE WHAT YOU ARE DOING, YOU WILL BE SUCCESSFUL.

-Albert Schweitzer

☐Drafted ☐Proofread ☐Published

Title: ______________________________

Date / /

Category: ______________________________

What kind of giveaway/freebie could I create to go with my most popular post?

Notes: ______________________________

☐Drafted ☐Proofread ☐Published

Title: ______________________________

Category: ______________________________

Date / /

What I Wore Today

Outfit: ______________________________

____

Accessories: ______________________________

Hair: ______________________________

Shoes: ______________________________

Makeup: ______________________________

How did it make me feel? ______________________________

____

____

❑Drafted ❑Proofread ❑Published

Title: ______________________________

Date / /

Category: ______________________________

Is there any affiliate programs I need to check out? List them below.

Notes: ______________________________

☐Drafted ☐Proofread ☐Published

Title: ______________________________

Category: ___________________________

Date / /

JUST BECAUSE SOMETHING DOESN'T DO WHAT YOU PLANNED IT TO DO DOESN'T MEAN IT'S USELESS.

-Thomas A. Edison

☐Drafted ☐Proofread ☐Published

Title: ______________________________

Date / /

Category: ______________________________

What product or service am I loving right now that I could write a review about?

Notes: ______________________________

☐Drafted ☐Proofread ☐Published

Title: ______________________________

Category: ______________________________

Date / /

What I Wore Today

Outfit: ______________________________

____

Accessories: ______________________________

Hair: ______________________________

Shoes: ______________________________

Makeup: ______________________________

How did it make me feel? ______________________________

____

____

☐Drafted ☐Proofread ☐Published

Title: ______________________________

Date / /

Category: ______________________________

What can I share with my readers about myself that will make me more relatable?

Notes: ______________________________

☐Drafted ☐Proofread ☐Published

Title: ______________________________

Category: ____________________________

Date / /

WRITING MEANS SHARING. IT'S PART OF THE HUMAN CONDITION TO WANT TO SHARE THINGS - THOUGHTS, IDEAS, OPINIONS.

-Paulo Coelho

☐Drafted ☐Proofread ☐Published

Title: ______________________________

Date / /

Category: ____________________________

What am I thankful for today?

Notes: ______________________________

☐Drafted ☐Proofread ☐Published

Title: ______________________________

Category: ______________________________

Date / /

What I Wore Today

Outfit: ______________________________

____

Accessories: ______________________________

Hair: ______________________________

Shoes: ______________________________

Makeup: ______________________________

How did it make me feel? ______________________________

____

____

☐Drafted ☐Proofread ☐Published

Title: ______________________

Date / /

Category: ______________________

How can I improve my writing productivity?

Notes: ______________________

☐Drafted ☐Proofread ☐Published

Title: ______________________

Category: ______________________

Date / /

THE SECRET OF YOUR SUCCESS IS DETERMINED BY YOUR DAILY AGENDA.

-John C. Maxwell

☐Drafted ☐Proofread ☐Published

Title: ______________________________

Date / /

Category: ______________________________

What is my blogs story?

Notes: ______________________________

☐Drafted ☐Proofread ☐Published

Title: ______________________________

Date / /

Category: ______________________________

What I Wore Today

Outfit: ____

____

Accessories: ____

Hair: ____

Shoes: ____

Makeup: ____

How did it make me feel? ______________________________

____

____

☐Drafted ☐Proofread ☐Published

Title: ______________________

Date / /

Category: ______________________

Looking back, what is my biggest fashion mistake?

Notes: ______________________

☐Drafted ☐Proofread ☐Published

Title: ____________________

Category: ____________________

Date / /

FASHION IS A LANGUAGE. SOME KNOW IT, SOME LEARN IT, SOME NEVER WILL - LIKE AN INSTINCT.

-Edith Head

☐Drafted ☐Proofread ☐Published

Title: ____________________

Date / /

Category: ____________________

What is one of my BIG goals? How will I celebrate when I achieve it?

Notes: ____________________

☐Drafted ☐Proofread ☐Published

Title: ______________________________

Date / /

Category: ______________________________

What I Wore Today

Outfit: ______________________________

____

Accessories: ______________________________

Hair: ______________________________

Shoes: ______________________________

Makeup: ______________________________

How did it make me feel? ______________________________

____

____

☐Drafted ☐Proofread ☐Published

Title: ______________________________ Date / /

Category: ______________________________

Where do you draw inspiration from for your blog?

Notes: ______________________________

☐Drafted ☐Proofread ☐Published

Title: ______________________________

Date / /

Category: ______________________________

I THINK A LOT OF JOURNAL ARTICLES SHOULD REALLY BE BLOGS.

-Nate Silver

☐Drafted ☐Proofread ☐Published

Title: ______________________________

Date / /

Category: ______________________________

What is my favorite post I've written to date? Could I do a follow up post?

Notes: ______________________________

☐Drafted ☐Proofread ☐Published

Title: ______________________________

Category: ____________________________

Date / /

What I Wore Today

Outfit: ____

____

Accessories: ____________________________________

Hair: ____

Shoes: ____

Makeup: ____

How did it make me feel? ___________________________

____

____

☐Drafted ☐Proofread ☐Published

Title: ___________________________

Date / /

Category: ___________________________

What is the best advice I ever got?

Notes: ___________________________

☐Drafted ☐Proofread ☐Published

Title: ______________________

Date / /

Category: ______________________

BE PATIENT, WORK HARD AND CONSISTENTLY, HAVE FAITH IN YOUR WRITING, AND DON'T BE AFRAID TO LISTEN TO CONSTRUCTIVE CRITICISM.

-Jonathan Galassi

☐Drafted ☐Proofread ☐Published

Title: ______________________________

Date / /

Category: ______________________________

What is my daily beauty regimen?

Notes: ______________________________

☐Drafted ☐Proofread ☐Published

Title: ______________________________

Category: ______________________________

Date / /

What I Wore Today

Outfit: ______________________________

____

Accessories: ______________________________

Hair: ______________________________

Shoes: ______________________________

Makeup: ______________________________

How did it make me feel? ______________________________

____

____

☐Drafted ☐Proofread ☐Published

Title: ______________________

Date / /

Category: ______________________

What creative way can I market my blog this week?

Notes: ______________________

☐Drafted ☐Proofread ☐Published

Title: ______________________________

Category: ______________________________

Date / /

THE STARTING POINT OF ALL ACHIEVEMENT IS DESIRE.

-Napoleon Hill

☐Drafted ☐Proofread ☐Published

Title: ______________________

Date / /

Category: ______________________

What inspired me today?

Notes: ______________________

☐Drafted ☐Proofread ☐Published

Title: ______________________________

Date / /

Category: ______________________________

What I Wore Today

Outfit: ______________________________

____

Accessories: ______________________________

Hair: ______________________________

Shoes: ______________________________

Makeup: ______________________________

How did it make me feel? ______________________________

____

____

☐Drafted ☐Proofread ☐Published

Title: ____________________

Date / /

Category: ____________________

How much effort am I willing to put in to make my blog a success?

Notes: ____________________

☐Drafted ☐Proofread ☐Published

Title: ____________________

Date / /

Category: ____________________

FASHION HAS ALWAYS BEEN A REPETITION OF IDEAS, BUT WHAT MAKES IT NEW IS THE WAY YOU PUT IT TOGETHER.

-Carolina Herrera

☐Drafted ☐Proofread ☐Published

Title: ______________________________

Date / /

Category: ______________________________

What are my interests and hobbies? Do my readers share the same interests?

Notes: ______________________________

☐Drafted ☐Proofread ☐Published

Title: ______________________________

Category: ______________________________

Date / /

What I Wore Today

Outfit: ______________________________

____

Accessories: ______________________________

Hair: ______________________________

Shoes: ______________________________

Makeup: ______________________________

How did it make me feel? ______________________________

____

____

☐Drafted ☐Proofread ☐Published

Title: ______________________________

Date / /

Category: ______________________________

If I could do anything, knowing I wouldn't fail, What would I do?

Notes: ______________________________

☐Drafted ☐Proofread ☐Published

Title: ______________________________

Date / /

Category: ______________________________

I MADE A DECISION TO WRITE FOR MY READERS, NOT TO TRY TO FIND MORE READERS FOR MY WRITING.

-Seth Godin

☐Drafted ☐Proofread ☐Published

Title: ______________________________

Date / /

Category: ______________________________

What unique experiences have I had in my life that I can share with my audience?

Notes:

☐Drafted ☐Proofread ☐Published

Title: ______________________________

Category: ______________________________

Date / /

What I Wore Today

Outfit: ______________________________

____

Accessories: ______________________________

Hair: ______________________________

Shoes: ______________________________

Makeup: ______________________________

How did it make me feel? ______________________________

____

____

☐Drafted ☐Proofread ☐Published

Title: ______________________________

Date / /

Category: ____________________________

Why is fashion so important to me?

Notes: ______________________________

☐Drafted ☐Proofread ☐Published

Title: ______________________

Category: ______________________

Date / /

WHAT YOU WEAR IS HOW YOU PRESENT YOURSELF TO THE WORLD, ESPECIALLY TODAY WHEN HUMAN CONTACTS GO SO FAST. FASHION IS INSTANT LANGUAGE.

-Miuccia Prada

☐Drafted ☐Proofread ☐Published

Title: ______________________

Date / /

Category: ______________________

What is one life lesson I had to learn the hard way?

Notes: ______________________

☐Drafted ☐Proofread ☐Published

Title: ______________________________

Category: ___________________________

Date / /

What I Wore Today

Outfit: ____

____

Accessories: ____

Hair: ____

Shoes: ____

Makeup: ____

How did it make me feel? ______________________________

____

____

☐Drafted ☐Proofread ☐Published

Title: ______________________

Date / /

Category: ______________________

What inspired me to get into fashion in the first place?

Notes: ______________________

☐Drafted ☐Proofread ☐Published

Title: ______________________________

Date / /

Category: ______________________________

THE DISCIPLINE OF WRITING SOMETHING DOWN IS THE FIRST STEP TOWARD MAKING IT HAPPEN.

-Lee Iacocca

☐Drafted ☐Proofread ☐Published

Title: ______________________________

Date / /

Category: ___________________________

What will you promise your blogging community this month and how will you deliver?

Notes: ______________________________

☐Drafted ☐Proofread ☐Published

Title: ____________________________

Category: ____________________________

Date / /

What I Wore Today

Outfit: ____________________________

____

Accessories: ____________________________

Hair: ____________________________

Shoes: ____________________________

Makeup: ____________________________

How did it make me feel? ____________________________

____

____

☐Drafted ☐Proofread ☐Published

Title: ______________________________

Date / /

Category: ______________________________

Who is my idol? Describe the conversation you would have if you had the chance to meet in real life.

Notes: ______________________________

☐Drafted ☐Proofread ☐Published

Title: ______________________

Category: ______________________

Date / /

JEANS REPRESENT DEMOCRACY IN FASHION.

-Giorgio Armani

☐Drafted ☐Proofread ☐Published

Title: ______________________________

Date / /

Category: ______________________________

In what ways can I give back to my community, either online or in person?

Notes: ______________________________

☐Drafted ☐Proofread ☐Published

Title: ________________________________

Category: ________________________________

Date / /

What I Wore Today

Outfit: ____

____

Accessories: ____

Hair: ____

Shoes: ____

Makeup: ____

How did it make me feel? ____

____

____

☐Drafted ☐Proofread ☐Published

Title: ______________________________

Date / /

Category: ______________________________

Brainstorm ideas for holiday posts?

Notes: ______________________________

☐Drafted ☐Proofread ☐Published

Title: ______________________________

Date / /

Category: ______________________________

FASHION IS A WEAPON THAT YOU CAN USE WHEN YOU NEED IT.

-Donatella Versace

☐Drafted ☐Proofread ☐Published

Title: ______________________________

Date / /

Category: ____________________________

What is my favorite accessory?

Notes:

☐Drafted ☐Proofread ☐Published

Title: ______________________________

Category: ____________________________

Date / /

What I Wore Today

Outfit: ____

____

Accessories: ____

Hair: ____

Shoes: ____

Makeup: ____

How did it make me feel? _______________________________

____

____

☐Drafted ☐Proofread ☐Published

Title: ______________________________

Date / /

Category: ______________________________

What statement do I try to make with my wardrobe?

Notes: ______________________________

☐Drafted ☐Proofread ☐Published

Title: ______________________________

Category: ___________________________

Date / /

YOU DON'T LEARN STYLE FROM WATCHING PEOPLE ON A RUNWAY. FASHION HAPPENS EVERY MORNING WHEN YOU WAKE UP.

-Shalom Harlow

☐Drafted ☐Proofread ☐Published

Title: ______________________________

Category: ___________________________

Date / /

What type of culture do I want to create around my blog?

Notes: ______________________________

☐Drafted ☐Proofread ☐Published

Title: ______________________________

Category: ____________________________

Date / /

What I Wore Today

Outfit: ____

____

Accessories: ____________________________________

Hair: ____

Shoes: ____

Makeup: ____

How did it make me feel? ___________________________

____

____

☐Drafted ☐Proofread ☐Published

Title: ______________________

Date / /

Category: ______________________

How will I attract new readers to my blog?

Notes: ______________________

☐Drafted ☐Proofread ☐Published

Title: ______________________________

Date / /

Category: ______________________________

THE SECRET OF GOOD WRITING IS TO SAY AN OLD THING IN A NEW WAY OR TO SAY A NEW THING IN AN OLD WAY.

-Richard Harding Davis

☐Drafted ☐Proofread ☐Published

Title: ______________________________

Date / /

Category: ______________________________

Who are my people? Where do I find them?

Notes: ______________________________

☐Drafted ☐Proofread ☐Published

Title: ______________________________

Category: ______________________________

Date / /

What I Wore Today

Outfit: ______________________________

____

Accessories: ______________________________

Hair: ______________________________

Shoes: ______________________________

Makeup: ______________________________

How did it make me feel? ______________________________

____

____

☐Drafted ☐Proofread ☐Published

Title: ________________________________

Date / /

Category: ______________________________

Write your best sales pitch for a new product/course you want to create?

Notes: ____

☐Drafted ☐Proofread ☐Published

Title: ______________________________

Date / /

Category: ______________________________

COMMUNICATION - THE HUMAN CONNECTION - IS THE KEY TO PERSONAL AND CAREER SUCCESS.

-Paul J. Meyer

☐Drafted ☐Proofread ☐Published

Product Reviews

☆☆☆☆☆

Product Name: ______________________________

Company: ______________________________

Thoughts: ______________________________

____

____

____

☆☆☆☆☆

Product Name: ______________________________

Company: ______________________________

Thoughts: ______________________________

____

____

____

☆☆☆☆☆

Product Name: ______________________________

Company: ______________________________

Thoughts: ______________________________

____

____

____

☆☆☆☆☆

Product Name: ______________________________

Company: ______________________________

Thoughts: ______________________________

____

____

____

Product Reviews

☆☆☆☆☆

Product Name: ______________________________

Company: ______________________________

Thoughts:______________________________

____

____

____

☆☆☆☆☆

Product Name: ______________________________

Company: ______________________________

Thoughts:______________________________

____

____

____

☆☆☆☆☆

Product Name: ______________________________

Company: ______________________________

Thoughts:______________________________

____

____

____

☆☆☆☆☆

Product Name: ______________________________

Company: ______________________________

Thoughts:______________________________

____

____

____

Index

EXAMPLE

Category: Finance

Pages 4, 16, 54, 60

Category: ____________________

Pages ____________________

Category: ____________________

Pages ____________________

Category: ____________________

Pages ____________________

Category: ____________________

Pages ____________________

Category: ____________________

Pages ____________________

Category: ____________________

Pages ____________________

Category:

Pages

Category:

Pages

Category:

Pages

Category:

Pages

Category:

Pages

Category:

Pages

Category:

Pages

About the Author

Who is Kaylee?
Kaylee always wanted to be a writer when she grew up, and now a lifelong dream has come true. She is a self-published author her first book in 2016. The title is "New Baby, New You" It's a book about resolutions to help the new mom.

Kaylee has been keeping a journal and writing in a diary since the first grade. She enjoys writing short stories and now, writing on self-help topics which is another one of her passions. She's always trying to learn and grow and wants to help others do the same.

She was homeschooled, along with her brother, which allowed her the freedom to start her small handmade invitation business, Kards by Kaylee, when she was just 17 years old.

She is married to her high school sweetheart, and they have started a family together. She is the mother of a fiery little redhead. She is thankful for a hardworking husband who provides for their family so that she can continue to work from home.

Having always been goal-oriented, entrepreneurial, and continuously reading self-help books, she is a wealth of knowledge. Her goal is to inspire people with her words.

You can find her blog at www.kayleeberry.com and follow along with her latest writing projects.

"I'm excited to grow my following and help other bloggers along the way." –*Kaylee*

Titles in the series "The Blog That Never Ends"

Available Now

Available January 2018

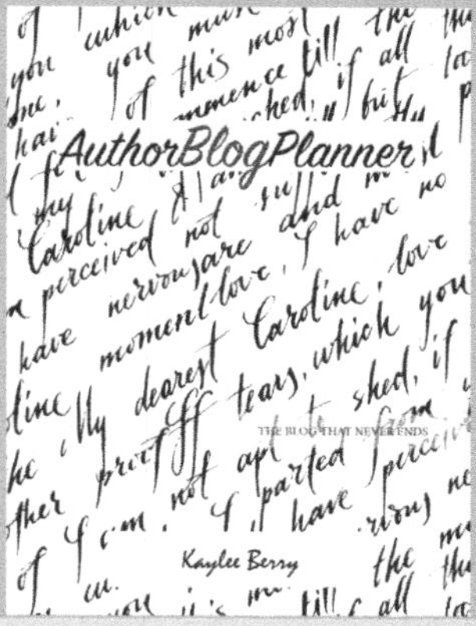

Minimalist Blog Planner Journal

DIY Blog Planner Journal

Fitness Blog Planner Journal

Made in United States
North Haven, CT
10 November 2026

22097468R00098